Naked Rain
Frozen in Time
A True Life Crime Story

by
Lorraine Taylor Ramkeesoon

Copyright © 2022 by Lorraine Ramkeesoon

All rights reserved. No part of this book may be reproduced in any manner whatsoever without written permission except in the case of brief quotations embodied in critical articles and reviews.

Paper Back ISBN: 978-1-7779977-0-0

-NOS NARRO PRO SILENTIUM-

"SPEAK FOR THE SILENCED"

EDMONTON POLICE HOMICIDE UNIT

"WITHOUT PREJUDICE WE SPEAK FOR THOSE WHO CAN NO LONGER SPEAK FOR THEMSELVES"

DR. GILMARTIN

IN HONOUR OF
JUSTIN ELLIOT TAYLOR
JANET SOM KANN
AND
JUSTIN JELIJAH TAYLOR KANN

> "THERE IS NO GREATER AGONY THAN BEARING AN UNTOLD STORY INSIDE YOU"
>
> — DR. MAYO ANGELOU

I would like to thank and acknowledge the following people:

Dr. Michael Ramkeesoon PhD Education (deceased)
Paul A. Taylor
Jamie Taylor
Jacqueline Taylor
Jennifer Taylor
Lisa-Anne Ramkeesoon
Lincoln Ramkeesoon
Michael Ramkeesoon Jr. (deceased)
Jahlisa Ramkeesoon
Ms. Clovest Walters
Molly DeLorenzo
Lydia Nasr
Celeste Bernard
Norman and Ruth Cummings
Edward (deceased) and Louise Kinakin
Gwen Woodworth
Dr. Anne Draginda, MD
Edmonton Special Victims Unit
Victims of Homicide Support Group, Edmonton
The Jury

FOREWORD

"Yah, Go Lorraine, go! " I remember shouting this as she zoomed ahead! She won the Track & Field race at our grade school while I came in last. We both were the kind to excel in any undertaking but I pulled a muscle and could no longer run.

We did however excel in our memorization of the poem

"The Hiwayman" by Alfred Noyes. How do you to learn such a long rendering as a child? Why by dancing and singing it! Lorraine has always been very creative and expressive and this book is a wonderful tribute to this quality.

I recall during one visit as adults, Lorraine and I got ice cream cones. We proceeded of the shop, ready to enjoy them when PLOP, Lorraine's scoop fell to the pavement! Lorraine was not annoyed and in fact, she saw the hilarity of it and we both laughed! This is Lorraine's take on life. She thrives on the humour as well as the blessedness of life's moments, and stores them in her heart.

Losing Justin could only have been intolerable and heart-wrenching, as Lorraine shares her and Justin's story.

Lorraine was born in Trinidad and moved to Canada as a child. She moved from Ontario and currently lives in Edmonton, Alberta. She has two siblings and is the mother of four. I have had the cherished pleasure of knowing Lorraine for over 50 years. Reading her and Justin's story reminded me of what a genuine, loving spirit she has. She encourages readers that having faith in a God who has a plan for us all, can provide the strength needed to make it through life's tragedies, knowing that peace will one day be ours to embrace. She will always be a blessing to me.

Gwen Woodworth

TABLE OF CONTENTS

Chapter 1:   Introduction: Christmas Part I
Chapter 2:   Family
Chapter 3:   Search Engine
Chapter 4:   Routine
Chapter 5:   East Coast East Side
Chapter 6:   Ode to Summer
Chapter 7:   Christmas Part II
Chapter 8:   Cataclysm
Chapter 9:   No Man's Land
Chapter 10:   Manhunt
Chapter 11:   P. T. S. D.
Chapter 12:   Descent
Chapter 13:   Bereavement
Chapter 14:   Voir Dire: Speak the Truth
Chapter 15:   Totis Viribus: With All One's Might
Chapter 16:   Sequela
Chapter 17:   Fin

Dr. Michael Ramkeesoon, PhD Education
(Justin's Grandfather)

In Loving Memory Of

Justin Elliot Taylor

Justin and Grandma

Naked Rain Frozen in Time

CHAPTER ONE

Introduction: Christmas Part I

As the snow curled from the heavens, it left configurations of diamonds in its wake. Indoors, Christmas was exploding with excitement. Video cameras were rolling, potpourri was simmering, hot chocolate was brewing and being enjoyed and oh boy, the gifts were being opened! Excitement was overflowing like a tidal wave building up to a great tsunami.

One of his presents was a book entitled "Long Road to Freedom" by Nelson Mandela. My son reveled in history, geography, poetry, and sports but most of all music. I mean, he read encyclopedias as a hobby and wrote music for fun. Upon seeing the book, his jaw dropped just like a mic. He said it was his best gift this Christmas! After all of the gifts were opened, and the fervor started to die down, he and his elder brother took off on a jaunt to spend a couple of hours with some friends. We asserted OK, see you later and they were off. It would be the first time in four years the whole family would be together for Christmas.

After Christmas, my eldest son and his younger brother made plans to meet and hang out together. A promise was made to spend some valuable, brotherly time before the holidays were over. A couple of days after Christmas, my eldest

Naked Rain Frozen in Time

son drove while they chatted and laughed. One of their shared passions was fast cars.

I remember when my youngest son was two years old, he would make these zoom zoom sounds and then giggle hysterically, repeating it over and over and over again. When he was three, his dad bought him a play motorcycle in fire engine red. My heart leaped through my throat when I saw him ride it down the six steps to the first landing and land on the wheels. He was ecstatic! I was horrified! He was banned from riding it for one week. The following week he got his motorcycle privilege reinstated and that little boy headed right back to the top of the stairs and away he went again. That was my first lesson in "boys will be boys". I should have revoked his license indefinitely.

"JUSTIN ON HIS RED MOTORCYCLE"

Naked Rain Frozen in Time

"JUSTIN MODELING"

Naked Rain Frozen in Time

"Justin Winking"

Naked Rain Frozen in Time

"JUSTIN TAYLOR: I LOVE CARS"

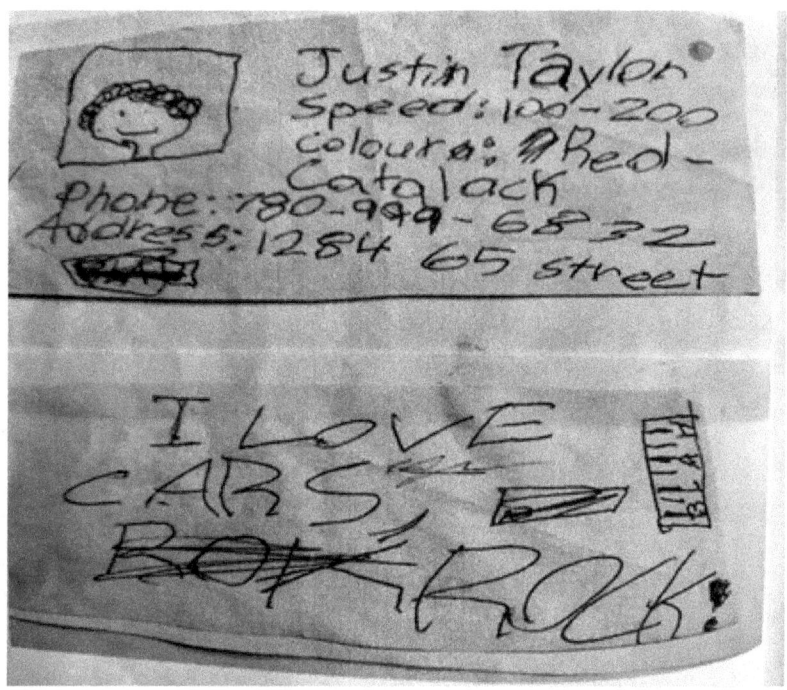

Presently, he being the younger brother, showed his big brother all of his old haunts. After riding around for a bit, he asked his big brother to drop him off at a friend's place because he wanted to pick up an Xbox. His big brother retorted "sure" and they parted ways with a "later"!

CHAPTER TWO

FAMILY

Christmas times were always a time for our family to get together and celebrate the birth of Jesus Christ as Christians. We were a happy clan of six. Outdoors, there was snowboarding, ice skating, road hockey, downhill skiing, snowman building, snowball throwing, and of course snow angels. Indoors there was always a Christmas movie or program or music playing. Our favorite family movie is "Christmas Story" with the famous line, "You'll shoot your eyes out!" There were games abounding and always a gym open somewhere for drop-in basketball.

One winter, in particular, we hit the slopes. My eldest son was the snowboarder and my younger son and daughter were the skiers. My younger son literally hit the slopes because he was confident he could navigate the diamond hill. He did great for a couple of runs and as life would have it, he tumbled and tumbled and tumbled losing his glasses on the way down. Well, he was OK but his glasses were MIA! So the guides snowmobiled up, down, and around the slopes with no success. Well, guess who had to climb the mountain to find the glasses? DAD!! His dad doesn't ski. Dad headed up the slope on foot, then gingerly slid down on his belly with arms outstretched in the snow. His hands caught onto something buried in the snow. Eureka! The glasses that not even the guides could find. Well, dad was a hero. A short time later we happily headed home.

"BROTHER AND SISTER ICE SKATING ON FROZEN STREET"

"JUSTING MAKING PANCAKES"

Naked Rain Frozen in Time

"OLDER BROTHER EMBRACING JUSTIN"

Naked Rain Frozen in Time

"JUSTIN GETTING A HAIRCUT FROM HIS DAD"

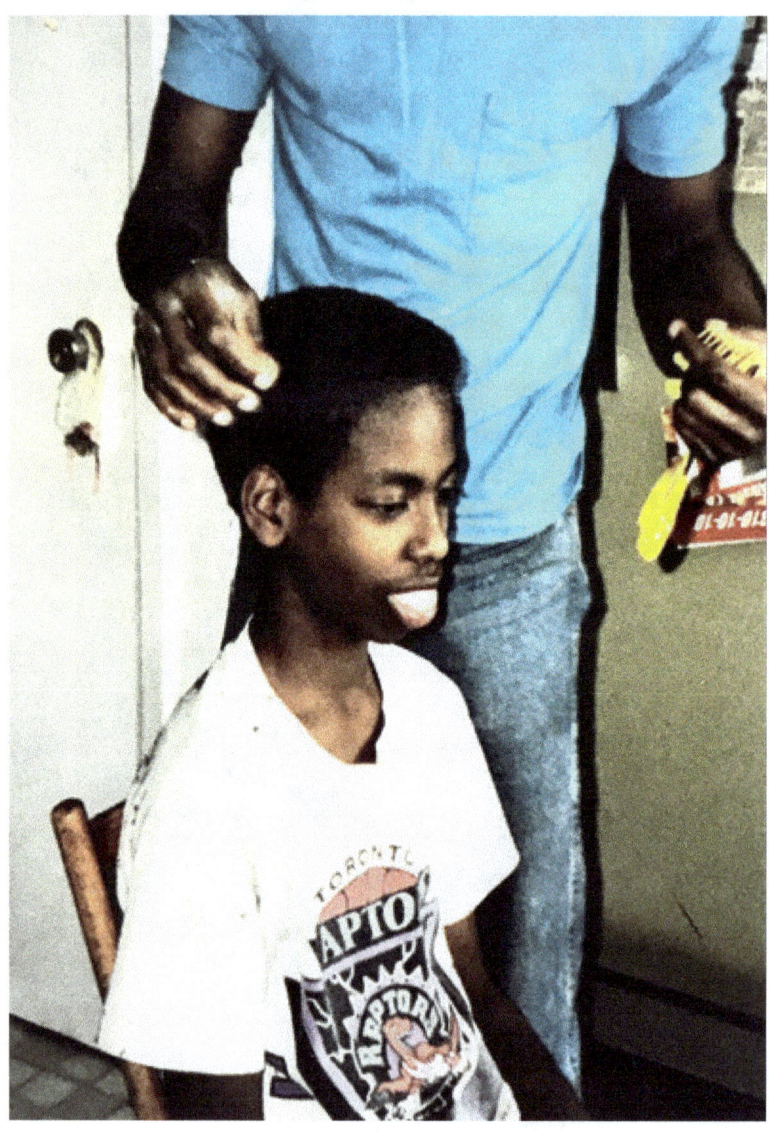

Naked Rain Frozen in Time

"JUSTIN HOLDING BASKETBALL"

Naked Rain Frozen in Time

"SHOW ME A HERO AND I'LL WRITE YOU A TRAGEDY"

F. SCOTT FITZGERALD

Naked Rain Frozen in Time

In 1984, my overnight bags were packed; one for mom and one for baby. Close to my due date, I slept through most contractions but one in particular startled me awake. I woke up his dad and told him it was time to head to the hospital. He hurriedly pulled himself together and we headed to the hospital.

It was very early in the morning when we pulled up to the emergency doors. Dad went to park the car as the staff got me into a wheelchair. By the time I arrived at the maternity ward, the doctor was ready to check me. Surprisingly, I was 5 cm dilated. I then told the nurses I wanted an epidural which was just as quickly, denied. I was then too close to 6 cm of dilation. I insisted upon it as the heavy duty cramps were reminding me of previous natural births. It was in my file that I was supposed to have the needle, but little did I realize I had managed my cramps so well thus far. I certainly wasn't ready to produce another 8 pound baby. The nurse prepped me for an epidural.

I bore a healthy, bouncing boy weighing in at 8 pounds, 7 ounces. In those days, mom and baby spent four to five days in the hospital after giving birth, to rest and heal. The nurses still bathed the baby and brought him to mom for breast or bottle feeding. Mom and baby had time to bond one on one. It was awesome!

Naked Rain Frozen in Time

CHAPTER THREE
SEARCH ENGINE

In earlier years, work was getting scarce in the trade industry in Southwestern Ontario. After the "Bruce A" nuclear plant in Kincardine, Ontario was completed, "Bruce B" opened up and was completed by 1984, the year he was born. His father also picked up jobs from Sudbury, Ontario to St. John, New Brunswick. In 2000, the pipe/steam/gas fitting industry almost came to a screeching halt. Whether it was the Darlington Power Nuclear Plant or the Toyota, Cambridge plant, it was slow. It was beginning to look for a reason to relocate. His dad started looking westward and after a lot of soul searching decided it was time to jump. He flew out to Edmonton, Alberta in the spring of 2001 full of energy, hope and the inkling of a new beginning. What a difficult decision to move halfway across this great land of Canada! We would have to leave our family, our life-long friends, our home and our church...our roots! We would be leaving behind a daughter! So for four months we planned, plotted and packed, getting everything organized for our relocation.

"LIFE IS TOO SHORT TO WAKE UP WITH REGRETS SO LOVE THE PEOPLE WHO TREAT YOU RIGHT, FORGET ABOUT THE ONES WHO DON'T. IF YOU GET A SECOND CHANCE, GRAB IT WITH BOTH HANDS."

Harvey Mackay

Naked Rain Frozen in Time

We arrived in Edmonton, Alberta on the eve of the third day of our travels to a flat prairie grassland. No rolling verdant hills and an unfortunate lack of colorful flora. Something I was unused to. But Edmonton has a harsh climate and what it lacked in scenery was made up by a magnificent skyline and some of the most extraordinary sunsets that would compete with any around the world.

On the cusp of this brand new city was a well-advertised restaurant. We stopped in, not before pulling our wearied bodies out of our vehicles and sliding into a booth. We ordered a meal and extracted our map. Upon deducing the location of our new home, and with filled tummies, we headed out.

We were going to locate our new home, being the pioneers of the Eastern clan to relocate to the Wild West.

Why were some traffic lights facing one direction but not the other? Why were there so many vinyl-sided houses? Where were all of the brick homes? Above all, no colorful sugar maple trees in August. How disappointing!

After a while, we discovered its own delightful and unique characteristics. We would learn to enjoy the summers because of their brevity, short and very hot; the early snows that would appear and disappear in autumn, flirting with us; the smell of winter on the horizon and the geese flying south; the flaming red bushes that would stride the roadways; the long, harsh painful winters that would last for months on end like we were on a tundra but, spring. Spring would burst through snow. Beautiful red berries would magically appear on the sumac trees and the buds would burgeon heralding new life. As with all of the seasons, spring would be inevitable.

Naked Rain Frozen in Time

LINES WRITTEN IN EARLY SPRING

"I heard a thousand blended notes,
While in a grove I sate reclined,
In that sweet mood when pleasant thoughts
Bring sad thoughts to the mind.

To her fair works did Nature link
The human soul that through me ran;
And much it grieved my heart to think
What man has made of man?

Through primrose tufts, in that green bower,
The periwinkle trailed its wreaths;
And 'tis my faith that every flower
Enjoys the air it breathes.

The birds around me hopped and played,
Their thoughts I cannot measure: -
But the least motion which they made

Naked Rain Frozen in Time

It seemed a thrill of pleasure.

The budding twigs spread out their fan,
To catch the breezy air;
And I must think, do all I can,
That there was pleasure there.

If this belief from heaven be sent,
If such be Nature's holy plan,
What man has made of man?"

William Wordsworth

Naked Rain Frozen in Time

Naked Rain Frozen in Time

My youngest son would eventually struggle in school because the Western School Board was unable to translate his grade nine credits from Eastern Canadian schooling. He would lose all of his grade nine credits and was now subpar to his peers. That became a serious deficit and deterrent to him at grade eleven. He was now one year behind his new colleagues. This in turn would eventually take its toll on his gentle, kind, sweet soul and spirit.

He became very discouraged and bitter but he kept his head high and his chin up. He made several new friends; some good and some not so good. He needed to fit in, a characteristic known to youths. He also met an abundance of beautiful girls that took to his quiet disposition and handsomeness. He was tall, dark and handsome. One girl in particular encouraged him to keep his spirits up and not let the poorly executed educational system strip him of his dignity. He was loved by these new Westerners.

Naked Rain Frozen in Time

HIS GROUP OF FRIENDS

Naked Rain Frozen in Time

"YOU ALONE ARE ENOUGH. YOU HAVE NOTHING TO PROVE TO ANYBODY."

Dr. Maya Angelou

Naked Rain Frozen in Time

CHAPTER FOUR
ROUTINE

Life continued to re-define itself. It moved forward expanding borders and boundaries. My children were growing up… they were young adults.

They were getting absorbed in their new lives and loves. And so was I. I was going to have to find a new career and new hobbies except reading, which was my one true love. I left behind the familiarities of croquet and badminton but I continued to swim and ice skate. I went on to learn downhill skiing on the bunny hills. The rush of traversing and the light snow kissing my face was exhilarating.

I learned how to handle an oar while white water rafting. As fate would have it, our raft hit a rock and upturned us. Shocking to say the least! Nothing went as planned. No one could find the chicken rope and the raft kept hitting my head as the life jacket tried to keep me afloat. As my renowned swimming champ and friend had cautioned me, if all else fails, do the dead man's float. Well you can't do any kind of float nor otherwise when you're trapped beneath a gravid raft. Whenever I bobbed up I took a deep breath.

Interestingly enough, my life did not flash before my eyes. I just kept trying to get from underneath it and at one point thought, "Well God, I didn't think it would end this way." What seemed like a few minutes later, someone got a hold of one of my legs and pulled me up. I was hyperventilating. I heard a man's voice say "stop breathing so hard"! WHAT??

Naked Rain Frozen in Time

He was trying to save face in front of his colleague. After I was able to moderate my breathing, I looked up and there was my champion swimming partner, doing the dead man's float. I couldn't believe my eyes. It had been a serious accident. The cold, wet drive on the bus back to camp, was numbingly silent. That would be my second and final white water rafting excursion.

Now zip lining is its own animal. I absolutely love it. Absolutely intoxicating. I started off as an amateur in the back country of Alberta and a few years later, was offered the chance to zip line in Antigua. Gliding through the rain forest was electric. I am looking forward to my next conquest in Niagara Falls, Canada.

I discovered a fabulous place to continue my love of horseback riding. Although the trails in Alberta are thrilling, they still lack the diversity of verdure I desire. After my last ride in 2019, my back was acting up too much and therefore I've had to leave that love at my heels.

I've had an offer to snow shoe. I used to snow shoe in Northern Ontario when I was about thirteen but not since. Perhaps one day… I brushed up on my French at a local university and dug in and still playing avec Francis. I would serendipitously find another career or as I would continue to live out West, discover that my career found me. I would start my new career a mere few months later embarking on a brand new life in Western Canada having left my family and friends behind. I would enter the field of Health Care.

Naked Rain Frozen in Time

During one of my usual commutes home from work one day, I vividly recall arriving home to something amazing. My youngest son had drawn me a luxurious bath. Upon opening the house door, I was surrounded by the smell of lilacs and roses. I took my shoes off and went up the stairs. I drifted towards the beautiful smell which was now emanating from the bathroom. Upon entering the dim lit room, my eyes widened in excitement as I saw all of the tea light candles surrounding the tub. I stepped away from the bathroom door to only become engrossed with these shy, warm, thoughtful eyes. I happily sang and hummed during my bath. I came out refreshed and revived after a long day. Was it Mother's Day I amusingly asked myself? Shortly after my bath, my son came up to me, hugged me and said "Mom you have the voice of an angel!"

Naked Rain Frozen in Time

"Thank you"

Dear Mom,

Thank you mom for giving me birth, looking into me... seeing what I was really worth. I'd never be perfect, but you taught me to try, molded this young man with high standards, like how I shouldn't lie. There was a day that I was born, and there's a day that I'll die but it's between you showed a love I couldn't possibly describe. I think It's called unconditional, please know this you're the only soul that keeps me emotional. When life had me feeling hate, and my eyes seemed so cold, I watched your reactions and so more love unfold. This love would never be matched, or its effect ever told, please remember how you've changed lives when you're 80 years old. It's been a little taste of heaven, having received your love, If I didn't know better I'd say you've ascended from above. Tonight is mothers' night, and I'd like to stay in your heart if I might..., Thank you for making my life so very, very bright.

Happy Mother's Day!!

Love always and forver,
Just T.

Naked Rain Frozen in Time

My son was very compassionate, thoughtful, loving, and caring. One day, a frantic neighbor rang our doorbell telling us her daughter had gone missing. Before the second blink of an eye, my son pulled on his sneakers while asking for a description of this little girl. He shot out the door telling the mom he was going to find her. He went through alleyways, the riverside, and under the bridge. The mother had notified the police that her daughter was missing even though it was less than twenty-four hours. Eventually, the little girl was found unharmed by police blocks away from her home. Indeed strangers had lured her into following them away from her residence with the enticement of candy. She was received into welcoming arms, unharmed albeit tearful, shaken and overwhelmed. She was returned home. She came back home...

One especially beautiful summery sunshiny day, my son found a baby bluebird egg in the backyard. He would have been around nine years old. It was in pristine condition. He built a nest for it out of sticks wedged together like the mama or papa bird would have done. Every day he went to the backyard to check on the baby blue egg. Until one day he looked in the nest and it was gone. He cared for it the best he could and was totally caught off guard that something he had loved so much would just up and disappear. We never found out if it was a predator that had grabbed the egg or whether it had hatched. Just the soft baby blue eggshell was left. He was very sad that he had lost his little baby robin. This would be his first taste of loss.

My musings once again take me to memory when he had brought home some sunflower seeds from school to plant in the backyard. He was instructed to plant it in the soil in a sunny area and water it daily. So every morning he would grab his shoes and hop outside to see if anything had transpired as yet.

Naked Rain Frozen in Time

This was his routine for the next couple of weeks until one morning he bounded outside to discover that some tiny green sprouts had been unearthed. Imagine his excitement as he discovered his ability to grow something!!! His sunny spot and daily watering had paid off!!! Well before you knew it, it was growing surprisingly fast. He kept watering it daily. By the end of summer, one sunflower had proudly grown to be an astounding six feet tall dwarfing him by about two feet. His excitement was contagious. He had brought something to life I pondered.

As a youth, my youngest son grew into a compassionate, empathetic, and altruistic young man. It's no wonder he started donating blood and working in a downtown soup kitchen.

Naked Rain Frozen in Time

"JUSTIN WITH ROBIN'S EGG AND NEST"

Naked Rain Frozen in Time

The following year, my youngest son had entered a science contest that was being held at Fairway Mall, Kitchener, Ontario. The contestants had to correctly identify a giant electronic device. He looked at the huge towering metal sculpture that was in the process of being built and decided that he would like to take a chance on this magnificent structure. It was under glass so that it would not be compromised. He entered his name.

Two weeks later, we received an official letter from the University Of Waterloo Science Department, informing us that indeed my son, was the first contestant to correctly identify the project. He received a commemorative coin as the first prize holder. He was ten. During these years there were lessons. There were music lessons, gymnastic lessons, swimming lessons, basketball lessons and skating lessons. My eldest son had started with the accordion in kindergarten. The following year he moved on to the tuba with the piano appropriately following. He also excelled in football and basketball.

My eldest daughter excelled at the piano with the especially classical piece "furelise". She was great with athletics including gymnastics and would eventually be preeminent at repartee and cooking. My youngest daughter fell in love with the violin after her obligatory piano lessons. She would also shine as a field hockey player and in drama. She would eventually be asked to go to the Julianne School of the Arts. I declined the invitation as I was not ready to lose my daughter to New York. My youngest son went for the electric guitar after his standard piano lessons. Boy was that amp loud!!! He would go on to write and make music.

The most beautiful part of it all, was that there was always music in the house.

Naked Rain Frozen in Time

"AT&T page dated April 14, 1994"

Imaging Systems

Global Information Solutions

580 Weber Street North
Waterloo, Ontario
Canada N2J 4G5
519 884 1710
FAX 519 884 9610

April 14, 1994

Ms. Taylor
Taylor Private School
20 - 25 Upper Canada Drive
Kitchener, ON
N2P 1G2

Dear Ms. Taylor:

I'd like to congratulate Justin Taylor for correctly identifying the product being built, displayed at the Engineering, Science & Technology Fair 1994. His was one of the first four names drawn who correctly picked answer 'B', the NCR 7766. His prize is a 1992 Commemorative Dollar.

Several students also helped create an object using our CAD (computer aided design) solids modeller. A plot of the final version, *Frankenstein*, is enclosed.

We enjoyed our involvement at this year's fair, and think these types of events are valuable to helping students understand some of the career options available to them. We hope all that attended the fair enjoyed and learned from our exhibit. Thanks for attending.

Sincerely,

James A. Michael
Mechanical Development Engineer

Copy: Martin Hynd, Director, Workstation Engineering
      Dave Bevers, Manager, Engineering Services

Naked Rain Frozen in Time

"University of Waterloo certification page dated November 29, 1997"

University of Waterloo

This is to certify that

Justin Taylor

has completed a continuing education course

Lego Dacta Workshop

at this University.

November 29, 1997
Date

Associate Provost
Academic and Student Affairs

Naked Rain Frozen in Time

University of Waterloo certification page dated March 28, 1998

University of Waterloo

This is to certify that

Justin Taylor

has completed a continuing education course

Electronics Workshop: Making Music

at this University.

March 28, 1998
Date

Associate Provost
Academic and Student Affairs

Naked Rain Frozen in Time

University of Waterloo certification page dated November 7, 1998

University of Waterloo

This is to certify that

Justin Taylor

has completed a continuing education course

Create Your Own Web Page

at this University.

November 7, 1998
Date

Associate Provost
Academic and Student Affairs

Naked Rain Frozen in Time

Every mom of young children from my generation went through similar familial adventures. There was Sesame Street, Curious George, Madeline Goes to Paris, and Winnie the Pooh (my youngest son's favorite) amongst others. There were books with accompanying cassettes for realism and sound effects like Strawberry Shortcake, Care Bears and Raggedy Anne, which were all time favorites at our house. As the children grew, our traditional shows became Anne of Green Gables, Road to Avonlea, The Sound of Music, Ben Hur, The Ten Commandments and The King and I. We had a fully phenomenal life and Winnie the Pooh never left his side.

Naked Rain Frozen in Time

CHAPTER FIVE
EAST SIDE EAST COAST

One day Justin's dad and II decided to take the family to the East Coast of Canada, as per our usual family vacations. We packed the minivan-like crazy. We felt the rush of **a v a c a t i o n!!** We left Kitchener, Ontario, and drove through historical Quebec on our way to New Brunswick. New Brunswick was absolutely verdant with wild flora and fauna. Everywhere you looked was green! It had lush rolling hills one upon another, hill after hill, valley after valley. At one point along the highway, there was a spontaneous spring outsourcing water from a secret place in the hills.

Sometime after arriving in New Brunswick, we had the extreme luxury of walking on the ocean floor in the Bay of Fundy. Extraordinary! The tide was out and we walked through caves that the water had tunneled out due to erosion. . A lot of photo opportunities! The tide came back in and from afar we saw the kayaks ducking to and fro on the swelling of the waves. Spectacular to think we had just been walking there!

Another day in New Brunswick, we witnessed the Reversing Falls. It is a place on the Saint John River where the water forces its way through a narrow gorge before tumbling into the Bay of Fundy. Twice a day, the bay tides push the flow of water to reverse against the tremendous and tempestuous prevailing current when the tide is high. What a phenomenon to witness!

Naked Rain Frozen in Time

Our next provincial stop was in Nova Scotia. We took a day and drove the Cabot Trail named after the explorer John Cabot. It stretches for miles and miles offering its expansive views of the Atlantic Ocean. On "the Trail" you'll find cranberry bogs and moose if you're lucky. We dined on various seafood dripping with flavors I cannot imitate. We visited Lunenburg, home of our very own Bluenose ship, represented on our dime.

The houses were of various shades of red, yellow, greens, and oranges. The lobster cages lay along the sides of various tributaries. Epic to Nova Scotia is Peggy's Cove, one of the most famous lighthouses in the world. It is magnificent in structure and stature. In Nova Scotia alone, there are over 160 historical lighthouses.

We stood in memory of the fallen on the Swissair Flight 111. We visited the plaque that commemorated the 229 lives lost there, in the deadliest McDonnell Douglas MD 11 accident in aviation history. My youngest son and daughter later sat on a piece of history conversing and contemplating life.

After eating our bellies full of lobster and butter at the nearby famous seafood restaurant, we were on to our next adventure.

We crossed the Confederation Bridge into Prince Edward Island. The Confederation Bridge is the longest bridge over ice-covered waters in the world. The country of Canada has so much rich history and interest, it was an absolute pleasure for our family to discover. Heading off the bridge into PEI, we stopped for a meal. We went for a post-meal walk and noticed something very unusual. The soil was red! This was the first time we had ever seen anything like it. We had been so naive as to the richness and diversity of our own country.

Naked Rain Frozen in Time

We picked it up in our hands and studied it like children. Of course, we discovered the island is formed from sedimentary rock which is very prevalent in our country. However, this rock is a vibrant combination with red sandstone which is high in iron oxide. No wonder the PEI potatoes are so good!

It was a dream come true for the kids when their eyes fell upon their very own House of Green Gables from the show, Anne of Green Gables. Talk about excitement! We received a guided tour of the house. They saw the bed that Matthew would have "slept in". They sat in a horse buggy for pictures. We got lost in the Haunted Woods.

"On the Ferry"

Naked Rain Frozen in Time

"The Haunted Woods"

Naked Rain Frozen in Time

"Peggy's Cove"

Naked Rain Frozen in Time

Naked Rain Frozen in Time

CHAPTER SIX
ODE TO SUMMER

Once again memories punctuate my thoughts... I think of quieter times...days at the cottage...

We made bonfires. We roasted marshmallows till they were burnt. And roasted wieners on an open fire never tasted so good! We would stay until deep into the night when the embers were dying down and the mosquitoes were biting through the chairs. Only then, would we wearily and pleasantly tired, call it a night.

The boys, big and small, caught and cleaned the fish. Moms took turns battering and deep-frying the delicious pike, bass, and speckled trout, using our various and favorite recipes. We had breakfasts of buckwheat pancakes every morning from the grill of our favorite chef served up with your choice of butter, maple syrup, and dream whip, or all of the above right on the beachfront.

We swam, canoed and paddle boated. The water was so inviting and refreshing and as clear as crystal. The children had all learned to swim from the myriads of lessons they had taken. So swimming out into the lake became second nature to them even though we never let them go far. The little ones always had to wear life jackets. Oh, we had so much fun and took so many pictures.

Naked Rain Frozen in Time

Mornings would bring happiness and hope with the birds singing. Warm days would lead to cool comfortable nights. Afternoons were spent either napping or reading or listening to the radio. Each family did their own midday sojourn.

One summer we spent in Lafayette, Louisiana visiting some of our family. We enjoyed the bayous, the museums, the Fairy Tale land with a giant shoe where the old woman lived with so many children, and the Nature Conservatory Centre. There, my youngest son was fitted with a genuine, giant turtle shell. He then proceeded to crawl slowly as though imitating the giant reptile but alas, the shell was quite heavy. We saw armadillos and alligators. There were also beehives with bees buzzing in and out of the honeycombs we were captivated by nature.

At one of the local restaurants, known for their amazing soul food, we dined on all sorts of deliciousness like jambalaya and hot pots. Some of us even tried frog legs. How posh! There was quite a quantity of seafood and all sorts of bean dishes, too numerous to mention. I tried collard greens for the first time. Louisiana has an amazing culture of Creole and Cajun which we thoroughly enjoyed.

The bayous were so humid and pretty with these trees with trailing branches all along the water's edge while some were in the water. They actually appeared very mysterious yet majestic.

We, in turn, invited our southern family to Canada. We packed a picnic basket of goodies and headed to Niagara Falls. The basket contained fried chicken, potato salad, fresh buns, sodas, napkins, cutlery, and a plastic checkered tablecloth.

Naked Rain Frozen in Time

It was voted the best picnic ever!! And I quote, my chicken was "the bomb"!

"PADDLE-BOATING: An older sister, Justin, and their dad"

Naked Rain Frozen in Time

"JAMIE AND HIS DAD HOLDING UP A LINE OF FISH"

Naked Rain Frozen in Time

"FAMILY AROUND THE CAMPFIRE"

Naked Rain Frozen in Time

Naked Rain Frozen in Time

"THE MIND COVERS THE MEMORY WITH SCAR TISSUE BUT IT IS NEVER GONE"

ROSE KENNEDY

Naked Rain Frozen in Time

Naked Rain Frozen in Time

CHAPTER SEVEN
CHRISTMAS: PART II

    While our sons were in the vehicle making plans for picking up an Xbox, they were also trying to arrive at a decision for meeting up in two days after my eldest son and his wife returned from Northern Alberta. His older brother and wife had to return to Toronto, Ontario to resume their post-secondary studies. Everyone wanted to of course make the best of the time we had together. It had been four years since we had spent Christmas together and what a wonderful celebration it was. It was above and beyond being special. Four Christmases! Moments were captured on video. Hugs and kisses are exchanged often. We poured over the fun times and fond memories we had had as a family in Ontario. We shared laughter and humor around the fireplace. We kicked back and enjoyed our hot chocolate doubling over with our eldest daughter's witty repartee. It was simply enchanting.

    The day had come for our boys to meet and enjoy each other's company. Two days had now passed and my youngest son had not returned home. Not only were we disappointed, thinking that he had chosen to be with his friends rather than his family, but his big brother was expecting him for a final visit before he returned to Toronto, and that time was quickly evaporating. They were supposed to spend some quality time together.

Naked Rain Frozen in Time

His girlfriend called us that evening voicing her concern that my youngest son had not been returning her calls and it was highly unlikely of him to do that. He was supposed to visit her on a Christmas evening as well. He did not show up nor had he returned her calls. His voicemail was full. His cell started dropping calls and accepting new voicemail messages but he never answered. Son where are you? I kept looking at my phone...

My son and his wife returned to Toronto. He flew back to Edmonton two days later not willing to let his brother's disappearance rest. He and his dad filed a Missing Person's Report.

An undercurrent of uneasiness and discomfiture was growing over us. Time was starting to lapse. Minutes were turning into hours and now hours were turning into days. Just to feel safer and useful, I decided to call the hospitals asking them if anyone fitting his six-foot-two-inch slender build had been admitted as a John Doe. Negative! Ok, that was a relief! I then called the non-emergency police line to speak to someone regarding my missing son. I was told to make sure and exhaust all of his hangouts his apartment, and his friends' homes. My mind was eased slightly when I was assured by the sergeant that young men have been known to just kick back and relax.

I didn't want to believe anything else. I needed to hope.

What is hope? Hope is the feeling that what is wanted can be had or that events will turn out for the best. Therefore, I had hope.

Naked Rain Frozen in Time

"Hope is the thing with feathers that perches in the soul – and sings the tunes without the words – and never stops at all."

Emily Dickinson

Naked Rain Frozen in Time

CHAPTER EIGHT
CATACLYSM

POP!!!!!

WHAT WAS THAT SOUND?

IT WAS LOUD!

IT WAS EERIE!

IT WAS DISTURBING!

IT WAS POIGNANT!

IT WAS SHARP!

IT WAS RIVETING!

Naked Rain Frozen in Time

All heads in the vehicle turned around looking for the source of that heinous sound. All but one...

Simultaneously, as the piercing, overpowering boom rang through the night air, the girl in the back middle passenger seat lurched forward and jerked the seat in front of her, the driver's seat.

Bloodcurdling screams superseded the otherwise silent night.

At evenfall, five young people embarked on a seemingly innocuous drive around the city of Edmonton. Little were the occupants of the vehicle aware of the sanguinary and sangfroid nature of that one person nor his atrocious state of mind.

Meanwhile, a crimson tide of tissue and blood seeped from a fatal wound. But not without it silently splaying on the passenger window, passenger seat, front seat, dashboard, and headliner.

With legs jerking and ears covered, confusion ensued. The driver yelled "What was that?" as she kept veering back and forth off the road. My son kept leaning towards her.

What the hell is going on? Didn't you hear that? Sit up and help me! She silently screamed. I can't control the car!

"Stay on the road" growled a deep voice from the back. She crushed to a sudden stop. The smell of hemoglobin permeated the darkness. Upon more inspection, blood had doused everywhere. It was on her face.

A gun cocked. "Be quiet" the dark voice menaced.

"Stay on the road and drive!"

Naked Rain Frozen in Time

She knew where they were, so she pulled back unto the freeway and exited unto a quieter road, farther away from the city, and closer to a Reservation. After what seemed like hours later, they heard "Help me with the body". He was talking to the other male passenger in the back seat. At gunpoint, the male passenger got out of the back and helped dump my son's body into a ditch, naked. The male passenger cried.

No one dared imagine what was actually taking place that night with their minds replete with all sorts of vivid scary nightmares.

Naked Rain Frozen in Time

WHAT IS JEALOUSLY?

Jealousy is a noun characterized by a state of fear, Suspicion or envy caused by a real or imagined threat or challenge to one's possessive instincts.

It may be provoked by rivalry, by competition or by desire for the qualities or possessions of another.

New Lexicon Webster's Dictionary

CHAPTER NINE
NO MAN'S ISLAND

Who bumped my seat? What were those smells? The thoughts crashed through the driver's head one into the other. Simultaneously yet broken thoughts. Jagged thoughts! Random thoughts! Abhorrent thoughts! As the five young people had driven into the night, an individual in the back seat of the car, poised his gun on his girlfriend's knee, and pulled the trigger. My son's hair parted as the shot rang out. As the shot pierced the cold, dark ominous night, the shooter's girlfriend's legs jerked towards the driver subconsciously. The driver felt her chair lurch forward and the young man in the passenger seat beside her, slumped towards her.

"Why aren't you trying to help me? Didn't you hear that sound? What's wrong with you?" "No one can sleep through that!" she inwardly analyzed.

No one said a word.

The killer repeated himself "I need to know where to put the body!"

The driver thought "What body? What is he talking about? Am I losing my mind? Who's talking? Why is he the only one speaking? Am I in a dream?" I'd better snap out of it and concentrate on driving. How had I been suddenly transformed into a paranormal state?" She had to rather some sense of reality.

Naked Rain Frozen in Time

"I'd better take us to a safe place where my family will help and save us" she thought. She pulled away from the side of the road towards a native reservation...

He didn't call to wish me a Happy New Year as he always did. I kept looking at my cell...no missed calls...no voice messages. His voice mail was always full... Finally I was able to leave another message.

I asked the machine,

"Where are you son? I need to hear from you. I am worried sick. "

Naked Rain Frozen in Time

"THERE IS NOTHING CONCEALED THAT WILL NOT BE DISCLOSED OR HIDDEN THAT WILL NOT BE MADE KNOWN."

LUKE 12:12 – The Bible

Naked Rain Frozen in Time

CHAPTER TEN

MANHUNT

His father and our eldest son retraced my youngest son's footsteps since we had last seen him. We recall that my eldest son had dropped him off at a friend's place where he was supposed to have picked up an x box.

After several consecutive stops proved futile, they then proceeded to a small community northwest of Edmonton, Alberta to his last known whereabouts after receiving a tip. It yielded negative results...until they found his car. In the glove box was the name of a woman who was responsible for the insurance. My eldest daughter traced the name and address online and over a two day period, I was able to finally reach her. She just so happened to be the driver.

LAW ONE:

"A STRONG INTUITION IS MUCH MORE POWERFUL THAN A WEAK

TEST"

By Siddhartha Mukherjee, Pulitzer Prize Author

Naked Rain Frozen in Time

I called her. She answered the phone.

"Have you seen my son?" I asked her.

There was great hesitation and then a quiet "No".

I asked her "Would you tell me what he was wearing the last time you saw him because you may have been one of the last people to see him?"

I didn't want to scare her away. Again hesitation.

She then proceeded to tell me "a white coat, green camouflage pants and white running shoes."

After that phone call to this woman, our sheer gut instincts told us we were onto something. My eldest daughter tried unsuccessfully to get a hold of her over the next few days and after much tenacity got through. My daughter asked her if she would come over to have a conversation about her missing brother. She acquiesced.

My children and their father met with the young woman and asked her some pointed and significant questions. After that stressful conversation, everyone realized it was time to approach the police with that new found information. What was about to unravel and be revealed would become one of the worst days of our family's lives.

Time stopped for me for one year. My family was about to be cast into CHAOS. Something passed over me telling my whole being that my son was gone. It was premonition. I pounded my right fist on the counter and screamed

"I STILL NEEDED HIM!!"

Naked Rain Frozen in Time

I slid down the kitchen wall detached and dumbfounded.

An RCMP officer (Royal Mounted Canadian Police) called our home and told his dad that his son's body had been found. He lay cold in death...tall, dark and handsome. Our son had been MURDERED!!!

And there lay the ugly, cold, grotesque, loathsome and repelling facts matched in its veridicality by the RCMP. Something a parent NEVER EVER wants to hear!

Immediately his dad started calling family and friends. My dear father passed out from the shock of hearing what had happened to his grandson. My brother and sister called back in disbelief to confirm the calls they had just received were genuine. His only surviving grandmother started making arrangements to fly from Ontario to Edmonton. His sister collapsed into her cousin's arms and was inconsolable. And his elder brother, well, he just fell apart.

His Eastern cousins cried in frantic mutterings, their words indefinable. One of my girlfriends also fainted after been apprised of the dreadful news. We were so close then that I had taught her daughter how to cook. Now one of her daughter's best friends was dead...The phone never stopped ringing after that.

One of the first persons to arrive at our home was a doctor and his wife. I just sat there looking into nothingness. He wrote out a prescription for me and his dad went to the nearest pharmacy to fill it. When he arrived back at the house, my friend Louise, handed me a glass of water and a pink pill on a spoon. I took the pink pill. It was a sedative...

Naked Rain Frozen in Time

The next day Lily and Beth from SPECIAL VICTIMS UNIT, came to our house to offer sympathy and emotional support. They presented me with a beautiful brown teddy bear wearing a big red bow around his neck. I was surprised but accepted it gracefully. I printed JUSTIN on the name tag. They spent some time with the family and pronounced, "Out of all of the homes we've visited, this one is the calmest." Perhaps it was the shock. Perhaps it was the presence of God. It turned out to be both.

RCMP FINDINGS

Interview of:	TAYLOR, Paul
Respecting:	TAYLOR, Justin Murder of
Conducted by:	Cst. Fred PEDLER Stony Plain Detachment
Taken at:	Edmonton, Alberta
Date & Time:	200

Naked Rain Frozen in Time

Interview of: TAYLOR, Paul

Q denotes Cst. PEDLAR
A denotes Paul TAYLOR

Q: Well I have some very bad news for you and I think you may know already.
A: Yeah.

Q: Your son's body was found yesterday on the Enoch Reserve just west of the city we've kind of got a lot on the go right now as to you know, exactly what happened and who might have done this. There's a number of people that we're looking for. And I know you were into the city police station, provided a brief statement.
A: Um hum.

Q: I think you had heard that this had happened eh?
A: Yeah. Pretty accurate what I heard actually.

Q: Yeah. If you feel up to it Paul, could we kinda go back a little bit like I noticed here you said that ~~Jason~~ Justin had been with you for Christmas.
A: Yeah.

Q: And maybe if you could, is there anything you can add, you said he was with you for dinner at Christmas.
A: Yeah, he was supposed to come back...

Q: He left on Boxing day...
A: to come back and...

Q: and that was with his girlfriend?
A: yeah.

Q: Do you know his girlfriend's name?
A: (unintel) she's expecting his child.

Q: Okay. Is that ████?
A: No, not ████ ████ is his other girlfriend.

Q: Oh okay. Okay so you can't remember this...
A: Well we've only come to know her in the last few weeks there before that I'd only seen her maybe 2 or 3 times.

Q: Okay.

Naked Rain Frozen in Time

Interview of: TAYLOR, Paul

A: Last few weeks you know since she's expecting and that. My brain is just foggy with all the...

Q: Yeah. Did she say, did his girlfriend say, or you mentioned here that she had called...
A: Yeah.

Q: and concerned that she hadn't heard from him.
A: Yeah. We're trying to call him every day.

Q: Okay.
A: Since Boxing day.

Q: Okay.
A: And I couldn't get him and I called her. And she called back and she said, where's Justin like can I, you know, we haven't seen him and he usually calls or. And so then she called later in the week and she was worried about him. But we weren't paying much attention because he's done that different times, you know.

Q: Yeah.
A: Been hard to get hold of and he doesn't....

Q: You mentioned that you called an individual that he was associating with.
A: Yeah.

Q: Do you know that person, that person's name?
A: I don't know. We only know him by the name, Dray.

Q: Tray?
A: Dray.

Q: Dray, okay.
A: Yeah, he was in Ontario all the time visiting his son so.

Q: So okay.
A: He wasn't around.

Q: But you were calling a number that you had for Dray in Edmonton?
A: Oh no, my son called this fellow, C. That he was associating with but we heard after we were looking for him.

Q: Okay that was, yeah I think James mentioned in his statement. Yeah, I spoke to a friend of Justin's named Dray who told me he spoke to a friend of his who told

Naked Rain Frozen in Time

Interview of: TAYLOR, Paul

A: him a man named Chris said he killed Justin.
Um hum.

Q: He told him this today. So this was the 7th eh?
A: Yeah. And we found out most of this on Saturday when we went looking.

Q: Last Saturday eh?
A: Yeah. My son tried to call Chris, call Chris goes by the name "C".

Q: "C"
A: Said, where's Justin? He said, I don't know I haven't seen him and he tried calling him a couple hours later and the number was disconnected so I guess that sort of sent flags flying wondering what's going on.

Q: Do you know what day that James tried to get hold of "C" cause you remember the date that you spoke or that he spoke to Dray?
A: Um...

Q: Cause the 7th was Saturday.
A: He spoke on 7th but he spoke, he tried to get Chris, "C" maybe 4, 5 days before that.

Q: Okay. Okay so some time last week...
A: Yeah.

Q: earlier in the week.
A: The week, yeah.

Q: Okay.
A: Either earlier than that week or the week before that.

Q: Okay. Oh yeah, okay he says, I called Chris talked to him on the 7th of January. When I called back three hours later, the phone was disconnected. And Chris said that he hadn't talked to him in about a week. Okay. You mentioned here that he didn't show up for his ▇▇▇▇?
A: Yeah.

Q: Was he supposed to do weekends...
A: (unintel) yeah.

Q: in ▇▇▇▇?
A: Yeah.

Naked Rain Frozen in Time

CHAPTER ELEVEN
P.T.S.D

What had been that sound? That poignant, eerie, sharp, disturbing, and riveting sound?? It had been the sound of the gunshot as it rang through the air before hitting my son behind the top of this left ear, parting his hair before it lodged in his brain. The RCMP told his dad our son had expired about two minutes after he had been shot. There was more to learn about what had happened to our son...

It had started to become my reality that there was a funeral to plan. How did this happen? Why did I have to plan a funeral? How did I get here? Oh yeah, someone had killed my son. A friend of ours from our place of worship offered to take over the funeral details. He led us by the hand from one impossible task to the next. We went down to the funeral home and had to pick out a casket.

My scattered mind was able to focus on what would be appropriate for a young man. Paul and I chose a beautiful warm honey almond-colored one with gold accents. He would like that if he had a choice... The flowers atop the coffin would consist of white roses, white lilies, white carnations, white dahlias, white zinnias, baby's breath with a wonderful spray of greenery.

Back at the house, our home was being consumed by flowers, family, food and the cards started piling up. Why was

Naked Rain Frozen in Time

everyone here? Why did my home look like a floral shop? My mind started to float between numbness and reality.

I took a pink pill and I placed the other tablet under my tongue...

When the RCMP found our son, he was cold and still in death. His body had been preserved by the temperature. The officers said they had never seen anything like it! His body had not been disturbed by the animals nor the elements. He lay pristine in death, all six feet two inches, tall, dark and handsome. They covered his body with a white sheet and he was placed in a van by the coroner.

The autopsy revealed his death was caused by a gunshot wound to the head. He was muscular, lean, healthy, and in the prime of his life. He was 21...

The funeral director called and told us that our son was laying at the funeral home. We were jarred.

Naked Rain Frozen in Time

"EVERY DAY BEGINS WITH AN ACT OF COURAGE AND HOPE...GETTING OUT OF BED "

MASON COOLEY

Naked Rain Frozen in Time

CHAPTER TWELVE
DESCENT

As he had lain still in death, so he laid still in the oak coffin. I neared him slowly, painstakingly, desperately, unavoidably, and solemnly. I needed to see up close if it was indeed him. But as I approached from far across the room, I knew unmistakably and undeniably that it was my son. He was wearing the suit jacket that his dad had picked out for him. It was also his dad's favorite jacket. He was wearing his favorite tie. He was wearing a brand new pair of black shoes his dad had bought him. The horror of my nightmare continued. It was my nightmare to bear. No one can take your nightmare away from you. And my nightmare had continued…cousins were screaming "NO" as they realized their cousin Justin was the one in the coffin. It was horrible! We slowly made our way home from the funeral home, our very own funeral procession.

As we approached the house, we noticed some people hanging around outside. We parked and got out of our vehicles. The closer we got to the house, the more people appeared. Bright lights went on and microphones appeared. I saw a large camera hoisted on a man's shoulder. It was the press. They were trying to ask me questions. I didn't know what they were talking about. Who told them where we lived? My father placed a protective arm around me and led me to the front door of our house saying "We have nothing to say at this

Naked Rain Frozen in Time

time." Stuck somewhere in the door, beneath the night sky, the moon illuminated a pale pink rose.

We had to make a program for the funeral. I didn't want to make a funeral program because that would mean that someone had died. My son had died. On the front and throughout would be pictures of him as a young basketball player alongside his elder brother and his dad. My son had always looked forward to 3 on 3 basketball games, I reflected. We would have to pick out hymns for the ceremony. The hymns would be sung by a young adult choir from our place of worship. I chose "Morning has Broken" as his processional song. I just felt inspired to lead with this beautiful, solemn song, a long-time personal favorite of mine. The other hymns were: "God's Almighty Arms around Me", "The Solid Rock", "There Is Coming a Day" and his recessional "Crown Him with Many Crowns".

The morning of his funeral, he lay in the oak coffin, tall, dark and handsome. A single long stem red rose lay across his breast, a profound token of love by someone who had loved him dearly. We, his family, sat in the front row of the church. With heads bowed, and splintered hearts, we remembered that beautiful, sweet soul that was now gone. He was surrounded by family and friends all of whom filled the church to capacity and beyond. Our proof that he was well-loved. We didn't know at the time that undercover police.

Had attended the funeral because it is known in their circles that the murderer would attend to keep an eye on the circumstances. They stood around the church in suits, ties, and sunglasses. I was in too much grief to realize their purpose.

Naked Rain Frozen in Time

As we headed the processional, I would glance up every few seconds to look upon all of the grief-stricken faces. They were hurting too. As his casket left the great hall and came to a stop in the foyer, his friends were laying their hands on it, on him, not understanding what has happened. Young men just laying their hands on his casket and openly crying. I saw what my son had meant to them and my heart was glad that he was loved.

Naked Rain Frozen in Time

MORNING HAS BROKEN

SWEET THE RAIN'S NEW FALL, SUNLIT FROM HEAVEN

LIKE THE FIRST DEW FALL ON THE FIRST GRASS

PRAISE FOR THE SWEETNESS OF THE WET GARDEN

SPRUNG IN COMPLETENESS WHERE HIS FEET PASS.

MINE IS THE SUNLIGHT

MINE IS THE MORNING

BORN OF THE ONE LIGHT EDEN SAW PLAY

PRAISE WITH ELATION, PRAISE EVERY MORNING…

GOD'S RECREATION OF THE NEW DAY.

WRITTEN BY ELEANOR FARJEON
MADE POPULAR BY CAT STEVENS

Naked Rain Frozen in Time

I was led to the limousine, sat in it, and took a pink pill...

His pallbearers were Jamie and David Taylor, Michael Ramkeesoon Jr, Harris Distant, Junior Steward, and Adam Puddester.

He was placed into the white hearse by his pallbearers. He was in his final vehicle but this time it wasn't a fast car. He was going to be driven very slowly because we didn't want him to leave us. There was a two-mile-long procession. We had arrived.

We stood by the side of the opening where he would be placed. We had to physically bid farewell to our loved one, my son. His father, his brother, his sisters, his grandparents, his cousins, and his friends had to say goodbye.

I HAD TO SAY GOODBYE.

He was going to be put into the ground, surrounded by dirt and stones. Ironically, just as he had been found. The hole had already been dug. As his younger brother was being lowered into the ground, my eldest son would proceed to place his own leather jacket onto the top of the coffin which was extremely profound to us and all of the guests. That would be talked about for years to come. What a pure and grievous gesture! His brother was gone and he had taken some of Jamie with him, literally and figuratively. It was tremendously moving, surreal, and deeply painful.

It was a cold, blustery, and frigid day as I wept on my dad's shoulders. We stood there in numbness and incapable of moving, frozen to the spot. My son went into the ground...

Naked Rain Frozen in Time

We left unable to bring him home with us. When he was born, we were able to bring him home, swaddled in a soft warm blanket, with his bright, shiny eyes sparkling with the h newness of life. We had to make sure he had a car seat to go home in from the hospital. We had brought him into the world and were responsible for taking care of him.

Paradoxically, he was not supposed to be born. At the beginning of my pregnancy, I had a uterine prolapse. A nurse friend of mine listened over the phone to my physical symptoms as there was no internal pain. She said to call her the next day if my symptoms persisted. During the next night, I was fine. After I had been up for about two hours, my uterus prolapsed again. She said I should proceed to the nearest hospital. I did. I wasn't prepared for the news I was about to be given by the emergency room doctor. He said that because my uterus had been prolapsed for approximately three days, I should consider an abortion. The risk of infection was extremely high and there was no guarantee that I would have a healthy baby. I was taken upstairs to a room for immediate bed rest and to consider what the doctor had told me.

My husband left work and shortly thereafter was at my side and we discussed it. The viability of our baby. I was twenty-five years old and it was a very difficult decision to make for us as a young couple. Do we keep the baby or not?? Were we willing to take our chances on a possible unhealthy fetus and bring it to term? Our final decision was to keep the baby.

I had a pessary placed below my uterus and was on complete bed rest for four weeks. It was challenging rearing three other children especially being unable to pick them up and comfort them for that period of time. At forty weeks, I delivered a big, fat, and cute as a button healthy baby boy! My

Naked Rain Frozen in Time

Justin weighed in at a handsome eight pounds, seven ounces.

Our last bouncing baby boy! How could I not think that that was God's blessing? It was to me. He grew into a tall, dark, handsome six foot two inches young man.

Naked Rain Frozen in Time

HIS JOURNEY'S JUST BEGUN

DON'T THINK OF HIM AS GONE AWAY
HIS JOURNEY'S JUST BEGUN,
LIFE HOLDS SO MANY FACETS
THIS EARTH IS ONLY ONE.

JUST THINK OF HIM AS RESTING
FROM THE SORROWS AND THE TEARS
IN A PLACE OF WARMTH AND COMFORT
WHERE THERE ARE NO DAYS AND YEARS.

THINK HOW HE MUST BE WISHING
THAT WE COULD KNOW TODAY
HOW NOTHING BUT OUR SADNESS
CAN REALLY PASS AWAY.

AND THINK OF HIM AS LIVING
IN THE HEARTS OF THOSE HE TOUCHED...

Naked Rain Frozen in Time

FOR NOTHING LOVED IS EVER LOST

AND HE WAS LOVED SO MUCH.

BY ELLEN BRENNEMAN

Naked Rain Frozen in Time

CHAPTER THIRTEEN
BEREAVEMENT

Bereavement is an ancient Germanic root word meaning "to rob or to seize by violence". It means to leave desolate or alone especially by death. It means to be torn apart.

Medical bereavement is a complex experience; the actual loss and symbolic loss affect a person's physical well-being as well as emotional well-being. The symptoms include a change in appetite and weight; fatigue; sleep disturbance; nausea and vomiting; chest or throat pain; headaches and post-traumatic stress disorder (PTSD).

Grief is the reaction to loss.

Mourning is our public expression of bereavement.

MEDICAL DICTIONARY, ONLINE
MERRIAM WEBSTER DICTIONARY

Naked Rain Frozen in Time

"THERE'S NOTHING WORSE THAN THE DEATH OF A CHILD. THINGS NEVER GET BACK TO NORMAL"

President Dwight Eisenhower

Naked Rain Frozen in Time

I could not get out of bed. I had no courage. I had no hope. Does my son know that I'm broken? Can my son feel my pain? I wrote my suicide letter and hid it in the bottom drawer of the armoire. Then I went outside and sat on the back stoop. I suppose Justin's dad was wondering where I was because the door opened behind me. He said something but I didn't hear him. I had these black shadows on the peripheral of each eye. I was in darkness. He decided to tidy up the back yard. He started swiping at the long grasses that had started to accumulate due to lack of care. Then he started cutting down some of the small bare branches that were hanging low. After all of the swathing and cutting and chopping ended, I heard the lawn mower. I watched him as the mowed the lawn. We had remnants of an old shallow well which looked more like a fire pit. I watched as he maneuvered the mower around the round structure. I then watched as he went and fetched the weed wacker from the old shed. I don't remember anything else after that. I had lost my memory from that day, the day after Justin's funeral.

My friends called me. I spoke to them. But I don't remember our conversations. I'm sure they were there supporting and uplifting me. I don't remember much of anything anymore. I have no memories of anything that transpired after I buried my son. He unwillingly and accidentally broke my heart and it can not be repaired.

My kind and faithful doctor told me to go on. So I took the meds...the one with food...the one without...the one for under my tongue, the pink one, the blue one and the white ones. I did as my doctor instructed because she told me people needed me. I did this for one full year because I was told to. I had no recollection of this for twelve months. I survived because I was fed, took medication and slept.

Naked Rain Frozen in Time

Was it normal to not know who the current Prime Minister was? Was it normal to not know the day of the week, month or year it was? I was blocking out the trauma. What did he unintentionally leave behind for us? Well, all of the paperwork from the funeral home, the death certificate, the autopsy results, the sympathy cards, the leftover programs, all of which has been placed in a green nylon zip bag left with me from his final resting place. I called my dad crying "Is this all there is left of Justin?" He tenderly replied "No Lorr, he's in our hearts and minds. That's where we keep him".

How were we supposed to fill that huge hole he left in our hearts, our minds and our tongues ? How are we supposed to resolve the polar opposites of him having a miracle birth and sudden departure? How do we arrive at the answers? How do we draw conclusions? What could we have done differently? He's just gone. I just wanted to die in his place. He had so much life yet to live and a child along the way.

A loss is a loss. A mother can experience loss in many ways. Some are more shocking than others but indeed the loss is great. It can be Sudden Infant Death Syndrome; it can be carrying a child to term without a brain; it can be an accidental choking or drowning; it can be a miscarriage; it can be a vehicular collision including a crash, pedestrian, hit and run. It could be suicide. It can be murder. There are a plethora of ways to lose a child. At any age; at any moment; at any time. We don't get to manipulate our losses. But we get to be intimate with them. We get to exist with it. We become one with it. I have come to understand that a part of my brain fused my mind and heart so that I can now put one foot in front of the other and walk. Sometimes backwards and sometimes forward, and sometimes, not at all.

Naked Rain Frozen in Time

Our minds and bodies can fragment from the trauma. Stress creates physiological pain. The angst about it reoccurring is horrific. It will dawn on you in an epiphany that because you have lost a child, doesn't make you immune from losing another. That is the depth of sorrow. You may not be able to attend functions; events; funerals; have joy; sleep nor eat. It will take longer than you thought possible. Therefore, I took my bereavement into the trial...

Naked Rain Frozen in Time

Naked Rain Frozen in Time

"Justin"

Naked Rain Frozen in Time

CHAPTER FOURTEEN
VOIR DIRE: Speak the truth

I moved through the maze of the judicial process. I went to the preliminary trial where it was determined that there was enough evidence to go to trial. At prelim, as we sat in a row behind some of the court officials, from a file folder, slipped out a picture of my son on a stainless steel slab, with one of his feet poking from under the white sheet. It was just enough for one of my daughters to notice, whereby she gasped and left, and was unable to attend the full trial with jurors.

That had taken a psychological toll on her. My mind fogs out at this point any time I try to recall this event. My other daughter made attempts to be present at trial but was only able to make it a couple of times. The psychological toll on her. My mind fogs out at this point any time I try to recall this event. My other daughter made attempts to be present at trial but was only able to make it a couple of times.

One year later, I sat in the front row of a courtroom. My family and friends surrounded me. A small white pill was dissolving under my tongue. I watched the judge. I watched the jurors trail in; some with their faces downturned, some glancing at us, some looking at him. I watched the crown prosecutor and I watched the defense attorney. Then I saw him. The man that had murdered my son. He sat in the accuser box replete with attitude and animosity. He had on handcuffs and leg irons. He was in an orange jumpsuit. He didn't plan on getting

Naked Rain Frozen in Time

caught. I just sat there staring at him wondering what was going through his head. Wondering why he chose to subject my son to such devastation? Wondering, why he had left my son naked out in the middle of nowhere? He was too sick in the head to realize the chain reaction he had set into effect. His nugatory actions were going to be on trial. He pretended to be a friend to my son, and my son was unaware that this man was an inconnu, a stranger.

This stranger couldn't have understood the effect on my son's unborn child. The effect on my son's father. The effect on my son's girlfriend. The effect on my son's siblings. The effect on my son's grandparents. The effect on my son's nieces and nephews. The effect on my son's cousins. The effect on my son's friends here in Alberta, in Ontario and the East Coast. The effect on me. The effect on the four other occupants of the vehicle. The interstitial domino effect he had commenced began the day he shot my son.

He had bragged in the remand that he was going to get a sentence of two years less time spent in remand. He spoke unintelligently to his peers in remand how he would get away with it. He had a pugnacious character which was at the heart of his actions. Little did he know, that in the following two weeks of trial, eighty-five witnesses were prepared to testify against him. Testimony from his ex-girlfriend to the driver of the vehicle to the other passengers in the back seat to the farmer...

 My son would never have entered the vehicle and sat in the front with this man behind him. Vicissitude was about to be this man's future.

Throughout the course of the trial, he sat there ossified. And sometimes he smirked. His self-assured hubris was unshaken throughout the trial. There were no visible signs of

Naked Rain Frozen in Time

compunction. It was uncovered that the killer had propped his gun-bearing arm on his ex-girlfriend's leg. It was already loaded. As a movie, he took perfect aim, and shot my son in the back of his head, just above his left ear," execution-style", said the judge. The killer's ex-girlfriend testified that as she looked on in horror, she saw my son's thick hair part as the bullet sliced through it. Her body contorted as she watched what was taking place. Her leg kicked in the driver's seat jerking the driver forward. My son slumped over unto the driver as he drew his last breaths. She screamed. The driver yelled at my son to wake up and help because she didn't understand what that loud "BOOM" was. My son lost control of his dignity as he expired. It happened so repulsively fast. The killer ordered the driver at gunpoint, to find a place to dump my son's body. After an excruciatingly long time, the driver redirected the vehicle to go out of town and head towards a quiet place named Enoch. It was a native reservation.

Upon arrival, the killer ordered the other male passenger, who was sitting in the back, shaking, to help him take my son's body out of the vehicle. He cried as he became the killer's unwilling cohort. My son was unceremoniously dumped. They stripped off his clothes. My son's nude body lay on the cold ground. The cryophilic environment would help preserve my son's body as a testimony and witness to what had occurred. He unknowingly became his own CSI investigator.

The driver was then commanded to leave the premises. The next day, he heralded her to a farmer's field. There, the killer dumped the gun in an abandoned trailer, not knowing he was being watched from afar. My son's belongings were burned in an oil barrel. The white coat, the camouflage pants, and the white sneakers he had last been seen wearing. To imagine this happening to my beautiful boy was beyond comprehension. The witnesses in the car would tell of how they were compelled to drive to a convenience store and car wash and that the driver, donning a black hoodie, would purchase cleaning agents including bleach, window cleaner, and cloths to purge the vehicle inside and out. Witnesses from the convenience store also testified verifying the purchases and the car is thoroughly cleaned.

The RCMP said the vehicle was absent of all biological substances. The RCMP also stated that this was the first case in their history, they had ever witnessed a crime scene that was void of any forensic or biological evidence. The case weighed heavily on eyewitness testimony.

Over the two weeks of the trial, we sat through evidence and testimonies. Eighty-five witnesses were waiting to testify, and one at a time, over the two-week period, articulated what they had seen and heard to the court. It was absolutely stupefying.

The farmer testified. The convenience store clerks testified. The driver testified. The male passenger testified. The killer's ex-girlfriend testified. The coroner testified. The crown didn't need to go through all of the witnesses. The preponderance of the evidence, what they had seen and heard about halfway through the trial, was going to prove sufficient.

The defense lawyer would try to sway the jury that it was possible that the other man in the vehicle, who was sitting in the back, could just as easily have shot my son as well. Remember, the defense only has to present a "shadow of a doubt".

As the trial was coming to a close, we presented our Victim Impact Statements. I spoke of his athleticism. He excelled in track and field. And how he used to read encyclopedias because he had a curious, brilliant mind.

Naked Rain Frozen in Time

I spoke of his love of music. He was working on a record label in Guelph, Ontario with his friend before we moved out West. I spoke of his love and compassion for others. He was thoroughly altruistic.

MY CURRENT VICTIM IMPACT STATEMENT

I can no longer conjure up his face nor his voice. I laid in bed for a year while my family brought me my meals and my medications to keep me alive. I was existing. I had written a suicide letter through my bleak fog telling my family and friends to forgive me for what I have done and I could not go on.

I became the essence of my who I am and I didn't know who I was. The essence of my identity had forsaken me.

And then I had to go to trial. I had to learn the morbid details of my son's last moments on Earth. How his thick hair parted as the bullet plunged into his brain. How he would lose control of his bladder and bowels as his life issued out of him. How his brain was splayed across the inside of the windshield. How his lifeless body was indignantly and disrespectfully dumped in a field. How his clothes were burned in a barrel on a farmer's field and he was naked.

How R G coerced the fellow passengers to participate in the bleaching of the vehicle erasing any sign or evidence that my son ever existed. How he callously called my other son to ask him how Justin was doing thereby casting any doubts that he was involved. There's been no remorse. How he threatened everyone to silence.

How do we reform such an individual? How was my son's life of such low value to his killer? How will anyone's life be of value to this individual? How do we go from him taking life to him not taking a life? How can this man be ever trusted in any community again?

Naked Rain Frozen in Time

Justin trusted. Justin was naive. Justin turned his back. Justin got shot.

Could that killer ever begin to comprehend how he had destroyed us, slowly, bitterly, profoundly, and abysmally? You lacerated our hearts, slashed a chunk off, nailed it back in, and said "deal with it!"

ANHEDONIA

THE INABILITY TO HAVE JOY;

LIFEFORCE LEAVES YOU MAKING YOU SLOW DOWN;

IN PSYCHOLOGY, IT MEANS THE INABILITY TO ENJOY EXPERIENCES OR ACTIVITIES THAT NORMALLY WOULD BE PLEASURABLE

Naked Rain Frozen in Time

"THE ROYAL CANADIAN MOUNTED POLICE ARE ALWAYS KNOWN FOR GETTING THEIR MAN"

CANDICE DELONG,

FORMER FBI PROFILER

Naked Rain Frozen in Time

CHAPTER FIFTEEN
TOTIS VIRIBUS: WITH ALL ONE'S MIGHT

My dad and I stood outside one day in the beautiful, bold, bright sunshine of the tropics conversing. We spoke of it being a nice day. Then, the sky unexpectedly opened up and an outpour of warm rain drenched our bodies. We stood there, mouths opened and clothing soaked and alarmed. There was no rain in the forecast. It was not the rainy season. Mother Nature and Father Time strolled hand in hand, maybe even smiling. Ironically, the rain felt and smelled good as it bounced off the bamboo and teak trees; the papaya, mango, and plum trees; of the coconut and banana trees; off the hibiscuses, chaconia, and Spain flowers. The leafy tropical land was revitalized and perked up willingly engaging the moisture.

We had just experienced NAKED RAIN. The unexpected... an unexpected moment, an unexpected event, and an unexpected phenomenon.

In many countries around the world, spring is inevitable. Snow gives way to frost and frost to dew. Spring is rolling in. The birds start peeping their light, airy lullabies. New life burgeons as the fragrant lilacs and honeysuckle blooms. Sometimes the perfumed scents are overwhelming. The butterflies eventually flit around gracefully lighting on and around the tall grasses and flowers. They bring with them a brief respite of calm and serenity. Then the bees come buzzing around busily

Naked Rain Frozen in Time

pollinating. I feel the soft, cool breeze stroking my upturned cheeks.

Renewal, revitalization, recreation, and reproduction. Yes. Another season is upon us.

Having Victims of Homicide Support Group was outstanding. It would be a season of respite for his dad and me during our mental anguish. At first, it was difficult to attend because we didn't know what it would entail and what the expectations were. It was suggested to our family by the Edmonton Police Services liaison for families that have undergone emotional and tragic trauma, specifically in our case, homicide. Justin's dad and I put one foot in front of the other and went to our first meeting. We were welcomed like family. We were greeted by soft eyes and shy smiles. We introduced ourselves and said who we lost. At some point in the circle, during the meeting, a smooth stone was passed from one individual to another. We were allowed to express any heartache, grief, agony, anguish, despair, malaise, and despondency. To our relief, everyone in attendance was in one of these phases and at the end of the passing of the smooth stone, we could open our hearts and minds regarding any feelings or hardships we wanted attention drawn to. If someone felt they could pass along any helpful information, they did. There were even people there that along their journey, found disappointment in our justice system. It was a unique and extremely helpful gathering and format.

After approximately three years of attending, we had been helped along our road to recovery which is still ongoing. I kept attending every once in a while to share and to listen. Eventually, I had written my first book, NAKED RAIN, which had drawn attention to the Edmonton Police Department. A few copies are now in their library.

Naked Rain Frozen in Time

    Time has passed slowly and quickly for me simultaneously. At times, I'm stuck in a quandary of shock and horror. At other times, it has slipped through my fingers. After I was home from work for a year, due to my inability to function, emotionally and physically, I was sent to see a psychologist by my employer. They cared and were very compassionate. Justin's father drove me to my appointment. There, I was shown the images for the Rorschach Test. I was asked the address of my appointment. I was asked who the current Prime Minister is. At the end of my session, he informed me that if people fail to go back to work at the end of one year, the chances they will return drop exponentially. I made a decision to return to work.

Naked Rain Frozen in Time

"WE MAY ENCOUNTER MANY DEFEATS BUT WE MUST NEVER BE DEFEATED"

MAYA ANGELOU

Naked Rain Frozen in Time

If we are blessed enough, we have the gift of family. The time comes with the grandest of gifts: grandchildren, which have been known to melt many hearts. My eldest son's firstborn came along at a whopping nine pounds. He was our precious grandson adding to the prosperity of my father's wealth, his great-grandchildren.

My eldest daughter's firstborn decided to be born in the USA. She was a beautiful, petite, sweet baby girl and very intelligent. Her name means Glory of God. I did wonder were we allowed to eat them?

Sometime later, my next granddaughter was born in Toronto, Ontario. I was supposed to be there for her birth but as fate would have it, she was going to be stubborn. I waved a teary goodbye from the cab leaving my very pregnant, sad daughter behind. I departed for my flight. It was a memorable visit because it was at the time of Toronto's brownout. It was an extremely hot summer and the air conditioners were whirring in the cold air. But the system collapsed from the high demand and all power over the entire city shut down. Imagine the audacity of the city to lose power right in the middle of the soap "The Young and the Restless"!

Something incredible happened during that brownout we went outside to see what was happening and whether it was localized or not. To our surprise, neighbors had come from the entire block and were socializing, each of us trying to figure out what had actually happened. A convenience store owner said he had heard that it was all over the city and the city didn't know when the power would be back up. They were trying to find the genesis of the event. In the meantime, he was thinking of ways to prevent his food from going bad.

Naked Rain Frozen in Time

The store ice was beginning to melt.

Meanwhile, we returned to the back of the apartment buildings to discover some neighbors started a barbecue. They were conversing, each one bringing out lawn chairs to join the circle. It was an amazing insight into humanity and how something negative can bring strangers together.

Our grand granddaughter the following week was safe and healthy. My third precious grandbaby, her name meaning Symbol of Peace, was born extremely artistic, in designing fashion and in dance. As time passed and we held them, hugged them tightly, kissed them repeatedly, and smelled them, along came grandbaby four.

I captured her birth on video. I was speechless. I was lightheaded I needed water. I put the camera down and a nurse brought me a glass of water and told me to sit down. After a few minutes, the lightheadedness passed. The nurse commented that she was going to end up with two patients in the delivery room, one having a baby and the other fainting. I leaped back up with the camera and continued to roll. My beautiful granddaughter emerged from the womb. She was going to be tall and athletic. New life again! How can one not be happy to see that? In Greek, her name means yellow as a canary and she is just as bright, sunny, and pretty.

My beautiful, continuing evolving family was expanding. We caught our breaths as the next grandbaby came along. He was a fair-haired Adonai born with a heart of gold and a gentle spirit. I was granted the gift of being present at his birth also. Another miracle! His name means God's Peace.

Naked Rain Frozen in Time

Before we knew it, another bouncing baby boy...my youngest son's child, named after his father. It was an extremely bittersweet experience. My son did not see nor experience the birth of his son. He left his girlfriend a single mom. But nevertheless, and in spite of, we continued to prosper. His name ironically means Justice.

The next ray of sunshine came from my eldest son. Her name literally means Sunshine. She was born an intelligent, creative, and happy-go-lucky. She has a way of lifting your spirit and making you smile.

Lo and behold, a slightly red red-headed beautiful drama queen. OMG!! She's never in one place for more than thirty seconds. She bounces from spot to spot and jumps up and down in the same spot repeatedly. She's a gorgeous bundle of energy. She's always the life of the family parties and puts a sparkle in each person's eyes. Her name means From the Golden Meadow. How apropos!

And lastly to date, is the prince. A baby boy who is simply princely. He sits quietly. He eats quietly. He even crawled quietly. He quickly leaps onto his dad's lap whenever a ball game comes on. He now knows how to fist pump. But he's not easy to make friends with, only mom, dad, sister, and dog. He quietly rules the roost with his happy chatter and is catered to because he is the prince.

Naked Rain Frozen in Time

Naked Rain Frozen in Time

"DEATH ENDS A LIFE, NOT A RELATIONSHIP."

DR. ALAN D. WOLFELT, PhD

Naked Rain Frozen in Time

Naked Rain Frozen in Time

"I wanted to apologize for going over. I wanted to add the story of a time eight years ago. I and Justin missed a meeting at a conference here. As we walked back to the Gospel Hall, Justin asked me if I ever thought about where I would go in eternity. He told me he was thinking about being saved. What happened to Justin is a big reason why I ever considered my latter end. I believe he is in heaven. God bless"

A friend of Justin's

Naked Rain Frozen in Time

CHAPTER SIXTEEN
SEQUELAE

He's not in pain. Death feels no pain. He's free from the world's trappings of pace, avarice, and stress. I deeply pondered these things and for the first time since my son died, I discovered there may be some peace entwined therein.

I had a dream. He was in a red telephone booth. He called me and I missed the call. I could see him standing in the booth with white ear buds in. I reversed the call to the booth and he picked up the phone. I heard his voice. I was relieved. It was only then I realized he was letting me know that he was alright. He smiled his broad warm smile exposing a brilliant white smile.

In the light of this moment, I knew I had to consider forgiving the killer for you see, he had taken his body, but not his soul and spirit. Unbeknownst to the killer, he had catapulted my son into a better place. I call it Heaven. My son lives on in my heart and mind. I walk daily with that scar of brokenness, hurt, assiduousness and torment. And he can never be replaced.

Another white Christmas will come to Edmonton, Alberta, Canada. His namesake will spend Christmas with the family. His cousins will ensconce him with love and attention. He'll get tight hugs and wet kisses.

There will be joy and laughter from the grandchildren and cousins as they play and enjoy each other. Our family will be

Naked Rain Frozen in Time

united in love. We will not be physically together on Christmas, but we will be in our hearts, minds, and spirits, just a phone call away.

Naked Rain Frozen in Time

"PERFER ET OBDURA, DOLOR HIC TIBI PRODERIT OLIM"

"BE PATIENT AND TOUGH; SOMEDAY THIS PAIN WILL BE USEFUL TO YOU"

OVID

SURVIVING: A JOURNEY THROUGH GRIEF

BY

Edmonton Board of Health

WHY ME?

Why should this happen to me?

It isn't fair.

Why should my loved one die

when others keep on living?

This is normal.

Death is not unique, but your grief is, therefore there are no ready answers.

…but your questions are important, death brings up many questions, doubts, and concerns.

Asking the question why…

is part of your need to understand.

Understanding is part of your healing process.

DYING MAY NOT HAVE SEEMED EASY

BUT LIVING ON CAN OFTEN FEEL HARDER.

I CAN'T BELIEVE IT.

Naked Rain Frozen in Time

Do you feel unreal?

That no one understands and nothing helps?
Do you feel that nothing can ease the pain
and think of suicide?
THIS IS NOT UNCOMMON.
The pain is yours, and you feel alone with it right now.
This is natural, it is all part of a long process
called mourning, and you are grieving.
Grief is not an illness.

It is a natural, healthy, human reaction, which most
people experience after the death of a loved one.
Grief is part of the process of healing.
It is a normal response to a feeling of loss and major
change in your life.

The death of someone who has shared your life is a major event.

The closer the person was to you, the greater your loss will be.

THERE ARE NO RULES FOR GRIEVING.

GRIEF IS VERY STRESSFUL.

Naked Rain Frozen in Time

It is hard and painful work. It is a complex time of need.

The impact of grief is well known to affect:

your health, your behavior, your social life, your emotions, and your

religious and spiritual beliefs.

At times all these aspects may be mixed up together.

It may seem like a bad dream:

It does not seem possible.

It may seem easier to deny what is happening and hope

that it will go away:

This isn't happening to me,

it's just temporary.

We need to deny

We need to step back every so often to gather strength.

What you resist, persists.

GRIEF IS A STRONG EMOTION.

Do not try to ignore it, be intellectual about it, or rationalize it.

FEEL IT.

Naked Rain Frozen in Time

The funeral was not the end of your grief.
It was just the beginning.

Grief is part of a process in your life, which can be successfully faced and worked through.
It is very painful.

Experience the pain.
YOU ARE IN A STATE OF SHOCK.
NUMBNESS...
when you are stunned,
nothing feels real,
everything you do, you do in a daze,
you feel like an actor or a spectator,
you feel outside of yourself
as if you had switched off all of your feelings.
This feeling of numbness is how your body protects itself
and attempts to cope with all that you have to do.
...Pain and tightness in your chest-your heart may skip a beat
and you may feel short of breath.
You may sleep badly, if at all.
You may find it hard to concentrate.
You may feel restless and empty.

Naked Rain Frozen in Time

You may find yourself searching to do something one minute,

then have no interest in it the next.

You may have aches and pains you never felt before.

Grief is hard work.

It is no wonder that you may feel tired, irritable and constantly exhausted, hardly able to climb the stairs, no matter how much rest and sleep you get.

It is easy to neglect yourself physically. However, you are under

great stress. At such times you are more at risk of becoming ill.

Try to look after yourself.

Naked Rain Frozen in Time

"GETTING THROUGH THE MAZE"
A Guidebook for Survivors of Homicide

by Sue Simpson

The police may be aware of your loved one's final words or approximately how long it took your loved one to expire. They may have photographs post-death.

Be careful of what you ask for and be prepared for details you were not aware of. Ask only the questions you want to be answered. You are in control of how much information you go after. They are unaware of how much information you are able to handle, only you know that. Always have support with you.

The scene of the crime will not be released until the autopsy has been done and the cause of death stated.

There are several teams of police officers involved in the investigation. There's an Identification Unit, a Superior, and two teams of investigators from the Homicide Unit as well as the Medical Examiner's office.

WHAT ABOUT THE EVIDENCE?

The Toxicology lab does testing and issues reports on drugs or alcohol in the victim's system.

The Chemist lab does fiber comparison.

Naked Rain Frozen in Time

The Biology lab does DNA work comparing blood staining on the accused's clothing to the blood type of the victim or identifying the origins of a hair sample.

The Firearms section may attend the scene and be able to establish the trajectory of a bullet.

COMMON FEELINGS THROUGH THE TRIAL

1. **Fragmentation:** having two lives-courtroom life and a home life. Everyone gets to go back to regular life while you have to return home without your loved one.

2. **Suppression:** wanting to have an outburst. It is best *not* to have an angry outburst during the trial. An outburst, loud sobbing, and continuous crying should be as quiet as possible. You may be asked to leave the courtroom as it can be interpreted as trying to influence the jury. It's best to leave, cry, and come back to the courtroom.

3. **Intolerance:** The accused behaviors in court may offend or irritate you. Do not give in to this bad behavior.

4. **Discomfort:** There are ways in which you may experience discomfort i.e. hearing details by witnesses; the face of the accused; and sharing rest facilities with the accused's family. Do what you need to do to protect your heart and mind i.e. bow your head or look down; leave the proceedings for a short break; take any medication the doctor may have prescribed. YOU ARE NOT DESERTING YOUR LOVED ONE.

5. **Difficulty:** You may find it difficult to listen to some of the testimony by forensics. Descriptions described by forensics

or injuries inflicted at time of death described by the medical examiner may be too painful to hear.

6.	Shock and Surprise: You may be shocked and surprised by the intensity of the proceedings and revealed details. You may be upset that negative references are made about your loved one and that his or her character is attacked. The *defense* will try to destroy the credibility and reliability of the Crown witnesses. Do not be surprised by the formality of the courtroom.

7.	Fatigue and Exhaustion: Some days you may feel that you need a break from the courtroom. Do whatever you need to do. Consider having a support person to relay what happened in court that day. ALWAYS HAVE SUPPORT.

Naked Rain Frozen in Time

VICTIMS OF CRIME PROTOCOL ALBERTA

From the Province of Alberta Canada

POLICE INVESTIGATION

You will get information about Victim Services. ASK if you don't hear from anyone.

Call your local police station and ask for help if they have not as yet reached out. If you ask, the police will let you know how the investigation is going and if charges were laid, what the charges are the name of the accused. Please cooperate with the investigation. They will leave you a file number, the name of the investigating officer and their phone number. Use it.

Do not rely on the news nor press regarding your loved one. Get your information directly from the source (coroner, medical examiner or police) and it will be accurate.

POLICE

Naked Rain Frozen in Time

WHEN ARE THE POLICE INVOLVED?

The police are involved from when you report a crime until they lay charges and send the charges to the Crown Persecutor

WHAT IS THE JOB OF THE POLICE?

I)   They must protect life and property

II)   Prevent and investigate crime

III)   Keep the peace

IV)   Enforce laws within the geographic area where they have authority

WHAT DO THE POLICE DO FOR VICTIMS OF CRIME?

V)   Respond when you report a crime

VI)   Tell victims of crime about Victim Services

VII)   Tell victims of crime how to contact an investigating officer

VIII)   If asked, give the victim (survivors) information about how the investigation is going and tell victims when police lay charges

IX)   If a victim has safety concerns, help the victim understand what choices are available for staying safe.

Naked Rain Frozen in Time

UNDER THE "FATALITY INQUIRIES ACT"

The Medical Examiner sets out to determine:

Who died?

Where did they die?

When did they die?

Why did they die?

How did they die?

They are in charge of your loved one's body.

This information is available from the coroner's office upon demand. They will also send you a completed statement of the above information including autopsy results.

These final results may not be available for weeks or months.

They complete the death certificate. This is not free.

In our case, the autopsy determined that our son died on a certain date, as opposed to when the body was discovered. Therefore, the date on the death certificate was incorrect.

Naked Rain Frozen in Time

MEDIA ATTENTION

Your case may be the subject of media attention.

State your privacy concerns at this time.

Reporters may call your home directly. You can elect someone to be the contact for your family or on your behalf.

You may offer "No Comment" at this time.

SAFETY:

If you are worried about your safety, ask for help by:

Telling the police

Getting an emergency protection order

Getting a Queen's Bench protection order

Getting a peace bond

Getting a restraining order

Getting a firearm's prohibition order

Finding out the release conditions of the offender

Develop a safety plan

If you have safety concerns because of the sentence, tell the police, Correctional Services, the Crown prosecutor, or Victim Services. They can help you understand the choices you have to help keep you safe.

Naked Rain Frozen in Time

RE BAIL OR JUDICIAL INTERIM RELEASE

What if the accused gets released to the community before trial?

If there is bail, the police or Victim Services can explain the bail conditions to you and help you get a copy of them.

Ask that there be a "No Contact" order set in place if it was a violent crime. (The accused in our case was not given bail, he was remanded until the preliminary and trial)

Start preparing a Victim Impact Statement. This is *EXTREMELY* as it denotes what this traumatic event has affected you, your family and loved ones. The judge will consider it as part of the sentencing procedure. You have the right to ask the court to read your Victim Impact Statement out loud in court.

If you ask, the Crown Persecutor will tell you the date, time and place of the sentence hearing.

If you ask, someone from Victim Services will go with you to a sentencing hearing and help you understand the court proceedings. (We did that in our case)

Naked Rain Frozen in Time

"ALLOW LOVED ONES TO HELP YOU. DO NOT ATTEND PRELIMINARY HEARING NOR TRIAL ALONE. "

Lorraine

Naked Rain Frozen in Time

CHAPTER SEVENTEEN
FIN

Exploring Critical Questions for When Someone Dies

By

Alan D. Wolfelt, Ph.D.

Five Common Myths About Grief

Myth #1. *Grief and mourning are the same experiences.*

Most people tend to use the words grief and mourning interchangeably. However, there is an important distinction between them. We have learned that people move toward healing not by just grieving, but through mourning. Simply stated, grief describes the internal thoughts and feelings we experience when someone we love dies. Mourning, on the other hand, is taking the internal experience of grief and expressing it outside ourselves.

Myth #2. *There is a predictable and orderly progression to the experience of grief.*

Naked Rain Frozen in Time

Each person's grief is uniquely his or her own. It is neither predictable nor orderly. Nor can its different dimensions be so easily categorized. We only get ourselves in trouble when we try to prescribe what the grief and mourning experiences of others should be, or when we try to fit our own grief into neat little boxes.

Myth #3. It is best to move away from grief and mourning instead of toward it.

Many grievers do not give themselves permission or receive permission from others to mourn. We live in a society that often encourages people to prematurely move away from their grief instead of toward it. Such messages encourage the repression of the griever's thoughts and feelings. The problem is that attempting to mask or move away from grief results in internal anxiety and confusion.

They're not crazy, just grieving. And in order to heal, they must move toward their grief through continued mourning, not away from it through repression and denial.

MYTH #4: Tears expressing grief are only a sign of weakness.

Unfortunately, many people associate tears of grief with personal inadequacy and weakness. Yet, crying is nature's way of releasing internal tension in the body and allows the mourner to communicate a need to be comforted.

Crying makes people feel better, emotionally and physically. Tears are not a sign of weakness. In fact, crying is an indication of the griever's willingness to do the "work

Naked Rain Frozen in Time

of mourning."

MYTH #5: The goal is to "get over" your grief.

We have all heard people ask, "Are you over it yet?" To think that we as human beings "get over" grief is ridiculous! We never "get over" our grief but instead become reconciled to it.

We do not resolve or recover from our grief. These terms suggest a total return to "normalcy" and yet in my personal, as well as professional experience, we are all forever changed by the experience of grief. For the mourner to assume that life will be exactly as it was, prior to the death, is unrealistic and potentially damaging. Those people who think the goal is to "resolve" grief, become destructive to the healing process.

Mourners do, however, learn to reconcile their grief. We learn to integrate the new reality of moving forward in life without the physical presence of the person who has died. With reconciliation, a renewed sense of energy and confidence, and ability to fully acknowledge the reality of death, and the capacity to become involved with the activities of living. We also come to acknowledge that pain and grief are difficult, yet necessary, parts of life and living.

As the experience of reconciliation unfolds, we recognize that life will be different without the presence of the person who died. We also realize that reconciliation is a process, not an event. The sense of loss does not completely disappear, yet it softens, and the intense pangs of grief become less frequent. Hope for a continued life emerges

Naked Rain Frozen in Time

as we are able to make commitments to the future, realizing that the person who died will never be forgotten, yet knowing that one's own life can and will move forward.

Naked Rain Frozen in Time

TO SIR WITH LOVE

BY

LULU

THOSE SCHOOLGIRL DAYS OF TELLING TALES

AND BITING NAILS ARE GONE

BUT IN MY MIND I KNOW THEY WILL STILL

LIVE ON AND ON

BUT HOW DO YOU THANK SOMEONE

WHO HAS TAKEN YOU FROM CRAYONS

TO PERFUME?

IT ISN'T EASY BUT I'LL TRY

IF YOU WANTED THE SKY

I'D WRITE ACROSS THE SKY IN LETTERS

THAT WOULD SOAR A THOUSAND FEET HIGH

TO SIR WITH LOVE

Naked Rain Frozen in Time

THE TIME HAS COME

FOR CLOSING BOOKS AND

LONG LAST LOOKS MUST END

AND AS I LEAVE

I KNOW THAT I AM LEAVING MY BEST FRIEND

A FRIEND WHO TAUGHT ME

RIGHT FROM WRONG

AND WEAK FROM STRONG

THAT'S A LOT TO LEARN

WHAT CAN I GIVE YOU IN RETURN?

IF YOU WANTED THE MOON

I WOULD TRY TO MAKE A START

BUT I WOULD RATHER YOU LET ME

GIVE MY HEART

TO SIR WITH LOVE

Dedicated to our father, Mr. Michael Ramkeesoon (1933-2018)

Naked Rain Frozen in Time

**"Do keep writing, Lorr.
You are my best author"**

Dad

Naked Rain Frozen in Time

Naked Rain Frozen in Time

"Justin in his cowboy hat bowing out"

Naked Rain Frozen in Time

Naked Rain Frozen in Time

TRIBUTE

Printed in the USA
CPSIA information can be obtained
at www.ICGtesting.com
LVHW011047151023
761135LV00006B/724